Daniel McCosh

Aspire

Bibliografische Information der Deutschen Nationalbibliothek:
Die Deutsche Nationalbibliothek verzeichnet diese Publikation in der
Deutschen Nationalbibliografie; detaillierte bibliografische Daten sind im
Internet über http://dnb.dnb.de abrufbar.

Cover and Design: Claudia Habermann & Daniel McCosh

Herstellung und Verlag: BoD – Books on Demand, Norderstedt

ISBN: 978-3-7519-4431-1

erednet dit dieux lumi

Seascape

Marine serenity
In waveforms
Clownfish
Belched
From an anemone
On bubbles and
Jet streams
We watch
From the corals
Pink with
Excitement
Mussels
Flexing
Starfish
Living in
Symbiosis
Far away on land
Primates screech
Throwing their
Contribution
To Nature
Into our waters
I wish they would
Clean the pipelines

Eels

Watch them writhe
Watch them slide
Transatlantic cables
Under the sea
Waiting to wrap
Around your legs
And strangle and
Thrash and
Suck you in

The eel waits
In the murky waters
Eyes gleaming
They are
Slippery bedfellows…

…The hooks have to
catch
Just the right place
Between the eyes
For freedom's sake

But he's electric
In his marine oasis
Floodlit
From the bows
Poised and charged
He zaps and stings
The bubbles
And hawks
Arcs that jump the waves
Singeing the very bones

Anthrophony

The animals taught us to dance and sing
In return we taught beavers to howl
A stick in the damn – of dynamite, no less
Unsolicited and thoughtless

Lamenting into the moonlight
A partner and child lost
The survivor chills my soul
With the saddest wail

Aviation, a masterstroke of modern engineering
We log our noisy progress, the forest pays in (silence)
Our ears deaf to the changing soundscapes
The depleted chorus of the natural world
Far changed from a soaring song and dance

What sounds more phony?
Biophony
Geophony
Anthrophony
Listen …
… to the sound of the world around you

solium et dignitatis regie fastigium sublimui
otruisq; seyus tam virorum qui feminarum c̄
nostri regimeu roboratur excellentiori honore
otruisq; seyus nobiles status et eminentie c̄
ad premissa surgentes intuitum et volentes

Bird of Prey

Resting in the cathedral vestibules
The great huntress dreams of diving
Keen her sight and swifter in flight
She circles and stoops in infinite loops
The fastest and most deadly ruler of skies

Thin tapered pinions
That will change direction in a heartbeat
An avian camera shooting
129 frames per second
Her
Wild
Tooth
Strikes

Lullaby for a Lion

Sleep gentle knight
Tomorrow you may
Quench your thirst
For a new dawn
Roaming the Savannah
With the pride
Of a golden snare
Beating the hunt
Your sunflower mane
Tawny golden
Fawned and molten coat
Folded onto sinew
As you paw the air with *bravoure*

Rest those powerful limbs faithful one
Rippling with the strength
That fends troubles away
Enter your dream-kingdom now
Rise fearless and free
As the cub once at home inside your skin
Sleep softly now, Monsieur
Sweet rumbling giant
Tail fanning gently in the grass
Swishing, switching, swooshing
Silently snoozing
Rising and falling
He sleeps contented tonight

Barnaby

Barnaby bumblebee
Could never mind
His own beeswax
His monocle
Slightly askew
As he enquires
About the news
Late for tea
With the queen
Again

And he mumbles
And rumbles
And buzzes
About the price
Of pollen
And who is
Romping with who
In the cornfields

Oh barnaby
When will you
Shun the life
Of a wannabee
And return to
Our eternal garden?

Sunflowers in Sunderland

Without the factories
It could be
Newfoundland
A wonderland
Not an industrial
Wasteland

Sunflowers
Cutting through steel
Robots
Revolting
Tattooing sunflowers
On rebel assemblies
Becoming human again

A poet shouldn't
Cast a cloud on a town
To justify a rhyme
But to turn down
A snapshot
Of sunflowers
In Sunderland
Would have
Been a crime

Soundsmiths

Soundsmiths
Florian might
Have called the
Music workers
Cast in the
Industrious steel
Of Düsseldorf

The red lights
And the palm trees
On Mintropstraße
Still oscillate with
The Kling Klang
Current
Of tomorrow's
Fabrication

Music is
Eternal work

Mothership

From his mother's hip
He wanted to be an astronaut
And build ecclesiastical machines
Sail through the inner space of outer space
Breathing the cosmos in staccato

It's almost beyond human consciousness
Watching the earth, the continents and the oceans
Rising through the window
On this endless interplanetary journey
He saw the universe beyond planetariums, geraniums and
terrariums

Rockets fuelled by sweet water and not tempered with
uranium
The time travellers helmet lined with foil clipped with
crocodiles and a worn patchwork suit fashioned from
threadbare curtains

If all this seemed confusing, he hadn't landed back on the
ground yet.

When the robots come

We are not mechanical animals
No iron legs, no iron lungs
Just blood and flesh and highly strung
Nothing that's done
Can't be undone

There's a young one
Deciding futures
By numbers
And optimisation
The excitement
Will fade
With the realisation
That he will be a victim
Of the same optimisation
When the robots come

Pixelated

Parts of your face
Didn't make
The screen
The parts
That move
The muscles
That make me
Smile
Make me feel
That you are real
That I am real
That you are not
A reflection
Of a lens
Or an echo
Of a room
Frozen
In a room
No matter
How many faces
Fit this
Faceless
…

…
Face space
Timeless
Space time
Endless
Faceless time
Future gloom
An acoustic
Cinematic
Trick

I need
To
Hug
Your
Real
Cells
Not
The
.
(Still
Life
Pixels)

Mythical surf

We know here
That the ocean gives
And the ocean takes
away
But still the foam
Shows no mercy

How many men
Have been consumed
By the weight of
These waters
How many souls
Washed away…

…In the surf
In the spume
In a torrent
In a storm
Rolling
Over
Our
Heads

Only to bubble
Beneath the surface
For a generation
For an eon
For an epoch
Rising for the occasion
Of an eternity
As they count the
Scales on their skin
Glistening in the sun

Comme noe apz le deluge auria a œurer mist bors le tvail er fist facufice et planta la bigne

Night-time Serenade

Staring down the hammers
The many faces of the jazz pianist
Dishevelled, dismayed, dystopian, delighted despot,
diligent, delirious
A night-time serenade
Strolling through the park where
Linden trees have stood for centuries
It is indeed a pleasure to meet with the sound of a night-
time journey
The timbre of fireflies and silent fountains

The Cellist

Both a wise man and a boisterous soul
Fingers wrapped around his neck
To coax, cajole a rising undertow
At rest, head and shoulders poised
Ready for another slight of hand,
a sight of sound, gliding proudly
With eyes fixed on high fidelity
Headstrong men would compose symphonies for her
sympathies
But the cellist is consumed
In a world of wood and honey

Ave maria gratia plena domin$\bar{}$ tecum

Comme &c

As I me walkid in a may mornyng I harda byrd

sing Chorus as I me walkid in a may mor

Sleepless in Panama

Temperate among the vines
Stretching and yawning
Warmed by a
A fine gentleman's coat
Of moth and algae
Composting delicately under copperwood and cecropia
On his weekly retreat

There is magic in the body language
Of this Velcro friend
Through nurture and maternal warmth
Overcoming a fear of heights
Ascending the vines
Mistaken for indolent and lonesome
This sly Casanova
Patrols his triumvirate harem at night

Attentive with the 360 degree slew of a night-bird
But the suitors are gentlemen
His presence is enough to warn
Leaf-eaters are peaceful folk
And they respect each other's territories
Too meek to build highways

But there is more to his slovenliness
Than meets the eye
Than brown-throated two toes or three

Deep in the mangroves of Escudo
His cousin swims
A hundred deep, the pygmies
Emerging from 9000 years of evolution
Dwindling for lumber and firewood
Forgotten from warm homes
Rediscovered by enlightened hearts

The carriage returns

The carriage returns
And the bell tolls
An actor calling for the next line
A night watchman
Jangling keys in the mist
Footsteps echoing in alleyways
The glint of a gentleman's pocketwatch and an ice-pick
Hooves pounding the devil's work
Each magnificent swish
Splashing life into the moonlight sonata
He writes until the crack of dawn

Another Stolen Memory

Sugar-coated almonds and teeth still sticky with
candyfloss

Sausages and onions pungent in the cloying afterword of a
summer shower

Every year we meet in a festival of colours as the
aerodrome rises above the church spire in our quarter

Swingboats and pirate ships
The music lags behind at least a decade competing with
the shrieks of the raffle man and hyperglycaemic children

The plastic ducks will remain forever out of reach no
matter how we poise our rods

I still do not know until this day why the plastic ducks are
the same colour as the parasols dotted among the graves
as we leave the fair and stroll through the churchyard

Why would you need to lend the bodies shelter from the
sunlight now?

Realism

Each night
Straightening the frame
On the wall
On the nightstand
The bedstead
A makeshift
Hat stand
Eyes closed in
A balancing act
A hand stand
A summer park
A bandstand

Back in the room a
Suitcase
Loosely bound
With a leather
Tongue
Spewing old
Photographs
Covering holes
In the carpet

And when you wake
You remember
Realism isn't good for dreaming

Sundials

Learning to tell the time
For the first time on a summer's day
A face set in stone and yet free to cast a shadow
On the poor man's minute and the rich man's hour

Standing with arms open
Spinning wheel of waving hands
Marking the wise man's eternity
The hummingbird's wings
Beats a steady rhythm over the aging clockwork springs

Fresh from the field

Scythes whistling keenly in the fields
Proudly gathering the harvest
Separating the wheat from the chaff
Teaching us to taste old ways again

Honest living echoes through the farmer's market and
then it seems the price is right
An earthly scent filling baskets again and the fruits are
swollen with the kindness bestowed on the land

Ruddy cheeked and coated with clodded soil, uprooting
the treasured memories of trusted crops that have fended
us from famine, and later standing in the kitchen bringing
love to the family fresh from the field

1922

The coach drew to a sudden halt
At the side of the street in 1922
Where the automobiles of tomorrow
Faded into the echo of a future blight

He bore the weight of the night in his winter coat
With a fine tapping of his quicksilver cane on the
cobblestones he held the mysterious airs of a man of
industry and grand designs, a man of poisonous purpose
and intent
Emerging from the doorway, he machined a path towards
the waiting carriage

Unable to meet the challenge of eyes fixed with such
urgent fervency and impatience cast toward the lesser
man
Potassium magnesium sulphate set into black opals
igniting into a matrix of colours and propelling polite
enquiries:
Was he an alchemist or a vagabond?

How long had I stood on a street of emperors when
another eruption in time gave way to daybreak in 1722 as
Stall-holders and tradesfolk
Took their place in
The freedom of markets
Wagons bear the faint intrusion of hay and horse manure

Clara rejoices in the bracing air; a welcome relief from the
heat of the scullery
Soothing tired bones
In a fleeting temporal collision, the anomaly of strangers
who should never have met
I bid them well

Aspire

Aspire higher than ascension
The tension released
You are lightning, thunder
Rolling through the mountains

Hewn into the rockface
Steadfast and headstrong
Aspire to conquer
With peaceful persuasion
To love tenderly these petals
The crystal dew
Aspire to become
Authentically yours

p xpm dnm. Qube erplens sequat
oraco genalis in andienag Draco

Animabus quesimus domine
omnim fidelium defuctor oio
proficiat supplicancu ut eas t
a perans omnibus eruas t tue redep
cioms facias esse participes. Qui cum
deo pre t spu sco umis t regnas deus
p omnia secula seculorum Amen
Requiescant in pace Amen.

Commendacio. Requiem eternam. p

eati imma
culan in
uia: qui
ambulant
in lege do
mim. Be
ati qui scru
tantur tes
timonia
eius: in
toto corde exquirunt eum. on eiu.

Also by Daniel McCosh:

Escaping
Ausgang
Dream Factory
Da Capo

For more poetry magic, readings and The Poetry Snug
podcast visit: http://escaping.mccosh.de/

Acknowledgements

With special thanks to the British Library [1] for supporting public engagement with our cultural heritage by making the images printed in this book available in the public domain.

Image sources:

[p7] **Additional 18856** **f. 5v** Sun and moon
[p9] **Additional 28841** **f. 3v** Sea horses, snails and shells
[p12] **Harley 303** **f. 1** Imperial falcon
[p24] **Additional 18850** **f. 15v** Building of the Ark
[p25] **Additional 18850** **f. 16v** After the Flood
[p29] **Additional 60577** **f. 221** Sheet music
[p35] **Additional 22332** **f. 131** Poligonum aviculare
[p42] **Additional 71118** **F** A soul lifted up

_____

[1] (https://www.bl.uk/catalogues/illuminatedmanuscripts/)